# The Real in Hyperreal

## Debasish Chattopadhyay

BookLeaf Publishing

India | USA | UK

Presentation by *BookLeaf Publishing*

Web: www.bookleafpub.com

E-mail: info@bookleafpub.com

ISBN: 9789360943622

First edition 2024

*I walk on the hallowed ground of my Father,*

*Tapas Chattopadhyay*

# ACKNOWLEDGEMENT

I am profoundly grateful for the journey that led to *Real in Hyperreal*. I express my indebtedness to the countless souls who inspired, supported, and believed in this poetic endeavor. To my family, whose unwavering love sustains me through every stanza, and to my friends, who lend their ears to hear the whispers of my soul, and to my students, who encourage me to shower poetic lines every now and then. Special thanks to Dheeraa, whose feedback and encouragement breathed life into these words. To the mentors and teachers, Susanta Bardhan Sir and Prabodh Sir, who shaped my craft, your guidance is etched within each verse. And to the readers who embark on this poetic voyage with me, may these pages resonate with your truth.

# PREFACE

In the quiet spaces between reality and imagination, where dreams merge with the tangible, lies the realm of the hyperreal. "Real in Hyperreal" is not just a collection of poems; it's a journey into the depths of human experience, where emotions transcend the boundaries of the ordinary and dance on the edge of the surreal.

Within these pages, you'll find verses that speak of love, loss, longing, and the intricacies of the human condition. Each poem is a snapshot of a moment, a glimpse into the poet's soul, inviting you to explore the complexities of existence through the lens of lyrical expression.

As you immerse yourself in these words, may you find solace in the shared human experience, inspiration in the beauty of language, and resonance in the eternal quest for meaning. *Real in Hyperreal* is an invitation to embrace the magic of poetry and discover the profound truths hidden within its lines.

# TABLE OF CONTENTS

# Sonnet on Creative Intelligence

You think of the 'noise cancellation' feature
Only in your 'earphone box'
What about the noises of subconscious nature?
Can't think out of the box!

Prufrock can become modern Hamlet
Can 'Shantih' replace 'the waste land'?
Thousands of questions were asked to the eternal
Prophet
To discover the essence of the inner wizard-land.

The creative intelligence operating from within
Your eyes are open, so you are blind!
And you are seeking Him madly
In the competitive intellectual society!

The frame-house glitters; 'Bible' is in Belinda's toilet
'Home' suffers in darkness; we are still naked!

————————

# Human, at Home?

Ignorance is human's 'Graymalkin'
Always on beck and call to 'Ego'. Satisfaction!
Anything can be achieved by Mirandola's 'Man'
Development, deforestation, denigration.
Perfection?
Engineering the passion of neuroplastic behavior
To dress up with 'Emotional Intelligence',
Goleman's!
Foucault's 'power-knowledge' revolves like
'Foucault's pendulum'
To torque the hunger to conquer. At home
feelings!
Pandemic spread through to lock down the
superpower

'Clear stream' of Lucifer chiaroscuros into
'dreary desert sand
of dead habit'. Cold war!
The potential mask-man is no longer at ease
Nature nurtures itself, leaving humans in
dis-ease!

# Humanity

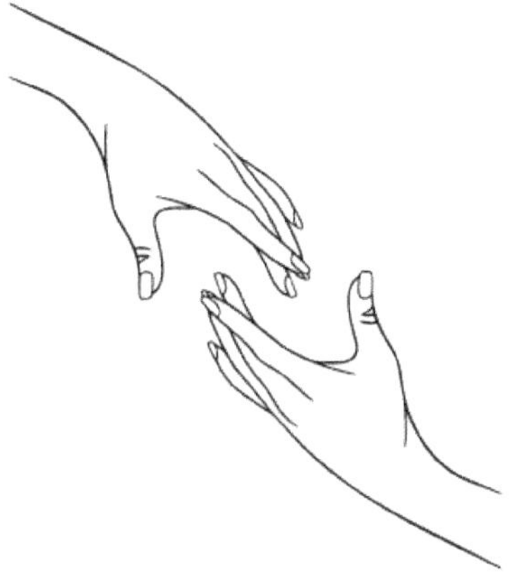

To be or not to be, that is the question
My dream provides me spiritual solution
A strange dream it was–
Krishna, Jesus, Buddha, Mohammad, Nanak
All came forward–
"We are the same soul, then why you all not?
Body is different but we are not.
Diseased mind becomes the cause of brutality
Realized soul is the fruit of radiant humanity."
Sprang up from the bed awfully
Meditation unlocks the dream peacefully
A sublime happiness glitter
Both in the outer and the inner
Humanity is the way to Divinity.
Being human is more than human being

Humanity enlightens the divinity within.
Let everyone understand the nature of humanity
Where life vibrates with potential divine glory.

# Ablutionary Eyes

You peep through my heart
Penetrate deep into your eyes
Thief-searching lamps are those
I am caught up!

Ablution in the ocean of love
Through the speaking eyes
Quite uncanny is the feeling
Still but restless I am!

Moving around for one glimpse
Your lamps brighten the heart–
Dark inhabitants are swept out
As You sit on the soul-bud.

I have changed like the clouds
Fly in my sky
Don't treat me as a caterpillar
Be my butterfly.

# Who am I?

Get out of my body
Wonder! 'Brave New World'!
Known and unknown encircle
Around me–
Doleful eyes.
Going to console them
Wonder! They can't see
Don't even hear my voice!
Eyes closed. Face dried
Limbs silent. Breathing evaporates
Lies the motionless!

Who am I?
Wonder! Dead I am?
But still alive–
Visible to none!
 Who am I?

# Love Cries in Cremation Ground

They burnt you down!
Listened not to my appeal
Your body was lost!

Clouds and lightning in my sky
I can hear inside the son's cry
Stars glitter in the outer sky!

You used hands to pull me up
I use mine to ignite You down!
My Love cries in Cremation Ground!

# A Sonnet on Birthday

Binary mind oscillates in apprehension amidst
celebration
Another year is added to the predestined
jurisdiction.
How much happiness is there on a birthday?
When you're coming nearer to Dooms- Day!
A sudden stillness saddens the inner happiness
When everyone is filling feelings of best wishes!
'Painful pleasure' gradually reverses into
pleasurable pain
A lot of heartfelt greetings will not go in vain.
Wheel of Destiny speaks silently how much we
live
And we ponder poetically how we celebrate to
live.
When attested affection finds the motion of love

Journey begins piercing the mind into the heart.
Life is a continuum, death an inn within to rest
Play the tactful tune of truth throughout without
rest.

# Sonnet of Colors

Soulful colors glitter within nature
Seven rainbow colors of human creature
Find vibration in each chakra-plexus
Vibgyor is in the firmament within us.
Color-bed is upon the soul-bud
Chakra-piercing rhythm pulsates gently
Elevation of mind like a Phoenix-bird
From red to violet, journey flows gradually.
The blue meets infinity in the Third-Eye
Sad-colored poet wears potential dye
Ecstasy is seen outside, felt inside
Colors being the ebb & tide, death & life.
Nature never betrayed the loving heart
Where two natures combined into a rhythmic
canvas.

# That World Map

Very late at night
I ran my fingers on
Its each part of the body
Gently, with Love.
Cried out vehemently–
"I am hurt. I am ill.
Blood is everywhere. Save me!"

I happened to find out
That world map
In a deserted dustbin.

# Stopping by Woods?

Are you thinking of a snowy evening?
Better think of a sunny morning
The 'woods' will no longer appear as 'woods'
Subtle frequency will be heard in
The inner mechanism of livelihood
They are not woods!
What if I call you a skeleton?
And praise your snowy beauty?
Your intellect will take care of
One of the 'Seven Deadly Sins' and
You become the most intellectual species!
Any difference between woods and forests?
The same as a skeleton and a body
The death in life and the life in death.
They are not 'woods'!

# A Sonnet for Teachers

A devoured darkness cried out in hollowness
Seven Deadly Sins creep into the mind of
ignorance!
Cholera breaks out, one to the other, within–
Is there any fighting force to work therein?
When the heart is pledged to the agitation of the
mind
Which divine blessings illuminate wisdom
within?
A ray of hope shines into the gateway of
stagnation

"Shiva" vibration reflects onto the way of
salvation.
The friend and the philosopher move forward to
guide
Everyone succumbs to illusion, a cluster of
darkness to hide!
A lot of patience to eradicate the pain of the
innocent
As sins sip into the mind and saturate to be
deviant.
Inner illumination removes the spell, mind
vibrates ripe
A teacher is indeed 'a sparking plug, not a fuel
pipe'.

# A Quatrain

Seven deadly sins lurking in the chiaroscuro
corner,
'Paradise' lost in Luciferian penumbra of
postmodern culture!
The 'hallowed' metamorphosed happily to be
'hollowed';
The most 'looked over' is getting 'overlooked'!!

# Black Beauty

I am a Black
I have no house to live
None to stand by my side
Have long been kept aside
Find no reason to survive!

I am not like you
Have no house but a home
Sleep not in a luxury bed
But in the lap of Nature
Don't hear noises of alarm clock, but
The strangely beautiful yelling of a peacock!

Our nature is not different
But the nurture, of course
You write beauty of nature

Never the nature within us!
Beauty can not be within 'black'?
Nature does ever create any lack?

In this 'cold' atmosphere
I'm sweating and sweating and sweating
Nature is not outside–
It is within.

# Postmortem of Postmodern Love

You told me you love the sun
And hid yourself in its mid-glory
Romanticized when about to die graciously.
You told, you love the sky
Bothered not during the spark in its chest
Wondered when the stars took wounded rest.
You told, you love the tree
Woodcutters mowed down mercilessly
You did not hear the bitter cry
You were busy counting its price.
You told, you love your best friend
Smiled when you needed his elevation
Your mirror broke the 'ship' after execution.
You told, you love your motherland
Wrote slogans for self-gratification
Forgot your sick mother provides nutrition.

I'm less amazed than afraid of "Love"
Where price is known; value unknown.
Your desire deserts – you love me too!

———————

# A Sonnet on Nature

The imagination brings forth a 'brave new
world'
Spring enters into blossoming nature
'Mind-forg'd manacles' smile on future
The air of love flows through the utopian world.

The snow covered the idyllic splendor of flower
Icy hands snatched the morals of John Gower
The boat convoluted in the pitch-dark tempest
No pendulum could put the pendulum at rest!

The solitary reaper sings in the offing
A tint of hope enkindles the sun within
The fog dispersed; Nature becomes divine
'If winter comes, can spring be far behind?'

Spring-year should remain in inner nature at
ease
Nature nurtures itself, all should live without
dis-ease.

———————

# Time

The best healer moving tick! tick! tick!
Eating up the bodies gradually
Encircling the clock and the cloak
Completes a life span!
Slow and steady wins the race!

The most valuable moving tick! tick! tick!
Undervalued until its final judgment
Quick era undermines slow movement
Death knocks at the golden old door
Slow and steady wins the race!

Humans open up a Pandora's box
God-centered universe is no more

Things fall apart, can the center hold?
Aggression is a quick mind's mark of trace!
Slow and steady wins the race!

Time and tide wait for none.
War is everywhere, outer and inner
The world is moving quickly with
Hatred, impatience, ego, suffering and death
Slow and steady wins the race!

———

# The Lament of Violin

The rhythm gently soothes the soul
Synchronized strings play the tactful tune
The tenor goes up in the mind
Strings break, violin is in the dustbin!

The girl grows up to be a woman
The innocence is lost in the world of
'Experience'
Love sells her into the institution of prostitution
Strings break, is the violin still beautiful?

Customers are happy in the strewn string
Can lustful fingers produce soulful music?
The life of death the soul is living
Tune of lamentation comes out of the violin.

"I'm not a girl, not a woman, only a prostitute
Violin no more, violation is played throughout."

_______________

# Carnival of Cadavers

The vibgyor is in the firmament
Nature is in seasonal decoration
Air is touching the heart romantically
Wordsworth visits again Tintern Abbey!

Eliot has come surpassing the waste land
The clouds encircle the color of the colors
The door is shut by the sudden gust of wind
Words of worth vanish in the voting colors!

The festival starts with the warmth of warming
up
Both hands meet to the people of both ends meet
Green, Red, Saffron hues define the nature of
humanity
Demons wake up to black the colors of divinity!

Educated potential knows the usage of uranium
Forget the universal potential of collective
equilibrium
Hunger for power turns them into voracious
zombies
Superstructure smiles above the heap of dead
bodies!

———————————

# Mindfulness

Life circle rotates in between
Seven chakra-plexus and seven deadly sins.
Is the mind only a Lockean 'tabula rasa'? then
How is the psyche integrated into Sister
Nivedita?
The intense power lies in the volatile mind
Hell and Heaven, versatile mind determine.
Conscious always dominates the subconscious
So he is unaware of the inner atomic colossus!
Hell and heaven are the states of the mind
Self-realization makes a human, divine.
When there is no 'sound and fury', no inner
debate
Into that state of freedom, let my countrymen
awake.

———————

# Disneyland

Life revolves around ambiguity
The only question is 'to be or not to be'!
Hamlet-situation devours the potential
Reality in itself becomes hypothetical!
Representations create the hyperreal!

We are lost in the Disneyland
Is Alice really in Wonderland?
Diversion takes us to a diasporic land
Robert Gilmore takes Alice to Quantumland
We all should realize our inner wizard-land.

---

# Exploration, 'Real' in the Realm

Wandering here and there to explore life
Read, learn, write poems to know and recognize
The significance of coming into this world
Fail again and again, life remains in a pseudo
world!
Hovering to get a glimpse of Paradise
Life ridicules playing the game of dice!
The war of Kurukshetra happening within
Abhimanyu is astonished & encircled therein!
"Life is a tale told by an idiot,
Full of sound and fury, signifying nothing?"
"Fool," said my Muse to me–
"You are blind as your eyes are open
Close the eyes, and you can see everything."

What to do when all the doors are shut?
Journey begins piercing the mind into the heart
The doors get opened from root to crown
Meet my 'Self' in the Paradise of New Town
The name, the body, the ego, the mind vanish
away
Life is within, macrocosm functions in
microcosmic way.
More's 'Utopia' is found, real in this realm
Ecstasy is dripping continually in the inner
domain
Krishna, Buddha, Allah, Jesus reside herein.

---

# Being Human or
# Human Being?

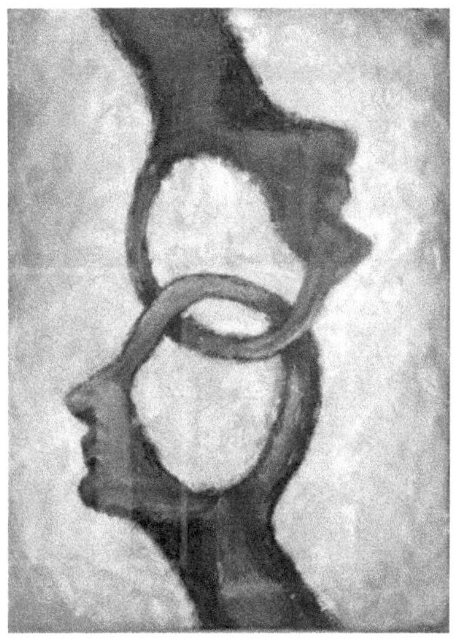

The vast world is a mystery
Tiniest is our existential reality
And we are the most intelligent egoists!
The ants are stern disciplinarians
The hyenas teach us togetherness
The trees stand for selflessness
And the intelligent species is merciless!
War breaks out–
Outside and inside
Atomic habits replaced by atom bombs
Insanity shakes hands with humanity

Colors divide the entire mankind
Eyes are fully open, still blind?
That rapist cut her body into thirty-five pieces
The rapist-artist artfully designs his
masterpieces–
Peace has been gracefully burnt in the
incinerator
'Pieces' have been divinely kept in a
thirty-five-liter refrigerator!
Voice of Judgement fades away before her
shrieking
Being human is more important than human
being.

# Infernal Paradise

Torrential rain, painful drops of the clouds
Terrible heat, burning tears of the earth
Treacherous humans, harbinger of death!
The heatwave winds throughout
The warmth is not the warmth of life anymore
Coldness prevails even in deadly temperature
Lively spirit sleeps in deadly life!
The gentleman is not a gentle man
The right side may not be right one
'Will' is only a future indicator
Caterpillar cannot be a butterfly!
Hyperreal clouds the mind in entertainment
Satan teases Eve; Adam is in bewilderment.
Infernal paradise is created by artificial man

The gentleman is not a gentle man!

# Emptiness

Full of sound and fury in each and every story
Hidden in silence the ecstatic divine glory
Life is not at rest, the dead rest in peace
Language signifies we are torn into pieces.
We are prudent, intelligent, and knowledgeable
Why we are here is still unintelligible!
God no more, it is human-centered existence
Justice cries in the offing, in silence!
'The west wind' becomes the destroyer
'Spring' is far away to be the preserver.
The scarecrow is dressed in modern fashion
'Things fall apart' to undress the civilization
The hollow men hover in chicken and egg
situation
Emptiness, in pursuit of happiness, death-bed
realization.

# Esemplasticity

I think therefore I am–
Reality or imagination?
Can a poet bring esemplasticity?
Creativity is the essence of neuroplasticity.
Fate dictates in the Greek culture
Character creates 'Fate'
Changing the inherent nature!
Men attained Godhood with divine imagination
Out-of-the-box thinking created the distinction.
Purity modernized into nudity
Sanctity metamorphosed into sexuality
Entity gradually leaves off divinity
Mind loses the calmness of serenity
Man has lost his potential identity
Rage, Revenge, Rape – the new reality.
Can a poet bring esemplasticity?

# SLIVING

We played with toys under the open sky

Love and laughter, our valuable treasure
The Gandhian smile was just a piece of paper
Weal and woe, the tender tenor in the piper.
We are now toyed with in the closed room
Love has become synonymous with lust
That smiling paper sweeps away gloom?
The axiom 'Dust thou art' bites the dust!
'Smile on' gradually reverses into 'smile at'
The most looked over now getting overlooked!
Price is highly valued, value is valueless
The less becomes high when it's 'priceless'.
Mirandola's man knows 'weal' is in 'wealth'!
Then how can 'ease' live with 'disease'?
Water is everywhere, not a single drop to drink

Living is everyone, sliving is what we must
think.

# LIFE

Darkness, intense one
Poems are not coming out
Life too–
Mechanical rhythm plays on
The tattered tenor horn
Forlorn–
Clouds betray the sky
Moss mocks at the pond
Mask hides the face
Ego covers the Man!

The river has lost its way.
Dead we are
Though beatings are on.

# Freedom

The bird is suffering in the cage
Golden one! Varieties of food!
Still trembling to get out.
For sixty long years
It is in this designed, golden cage.
It never tried to be free

Never longed for the wild forest
Never to swim in the river
Never did urge to live!
Can a cage be the 'room' to survive?
The body becomes old
The youth vanishes away
The colorful charm is a hoax?
Happiness is not in the golden cage
Glamor tricks and befools all the age
Death-bed thinks of life and freedom
The king is dead, unaware of his kingdom!

# FRIEND

Friends innumerable
In the digital era
He is known by the followers
The number of followers!
Still, he has none to look after!
He tries heart and soul
To increase the digital community
To set up himself as a superhuman
All the life spent in beauty and luxury
No friend to light up his inner treasury!
A friend in need is a friend indeed?
The golden age knows no axiom of age-old!
The smoke rounds away in the air

Drink, dance, death; twinkling stars glitter
The ship of friends sinks in colorful water
He has none to look after!
Digital voice shuts up the voice of Conscience
Our eyes are open, and thus we become blind!

# The Journey

Walking through the unmetalled road
Sea waves in the solid state
Zigzag road to reach the destination.
Still walking through the dense forest,

Dark lake, black airspace–
To meet You.
The coiled serpent sleeps dormantly
Narendranath awakens it gracefully
To become Swami Vivekananda.
Journey begins upward to meet the 'self'
In the dark, frowning forest without help!

Pitch-dark clouds cover the entire sight
Darkness is nothing, only absence of light.
Sitting still, eyes closed, darkness evaporates
The sleeping serpent awakens and radiates
Destiny's designed denouement dawns at
destination–
We all are one and should live in unison
Then why is here degenerated discrimination?
The intellectuals are lacking in self-realization!

# "Leave me to Live Together"

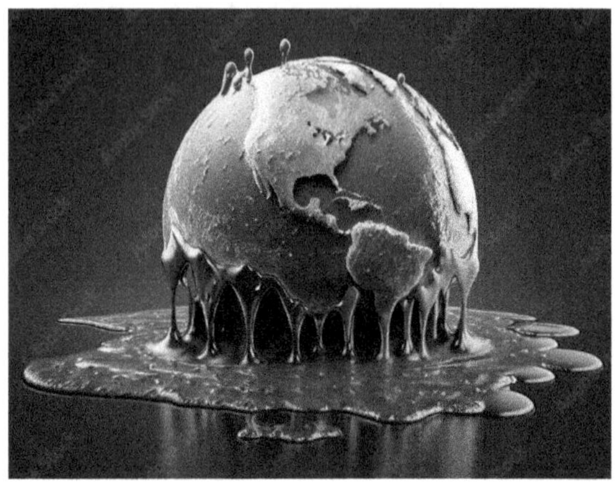

Blood is coming out
The flea is sucking gently
Flies are buzzing around
To get the share of the wound.
Horrible cry of our Mother–
"I'm wounded. Leave me to Live
Together..."
Mother Earth cracks up
Intellect rolls into the ground
The sea engulfs the ego
The west wind destroys the house
To preserve the 'home'.
The withered leaves are blown away
Winter is over! Nature nurtures itself
Humans are yet to find out lost humanity.

# Vision, De-vision; Peace, Piece

Separated by caste, creed, religion, and more
Vision no more, division visits door to door!
The cold warmth warming up the planet
The warm coldness conjuring up this decade.
White mind takes up red, green, saffron colors.

Black prevails throughout, lightning thunders!
Happiness resides only on digital platforms
Heart is venomous, Brain is left to dustbins!

The intelligentsia seminars on Dalit people
In the air-conditioned room–
Upgradation. Or degradation?
The air flows and the river blows!
Ego grows and the relationship flaws
Things priceless and Love valueless
'Peace' has been metamorphosed into 'pieces'.

# Religion and Realization

Blood flows through, the animal sacrificed
Before the altar of the universal Mother
Rhythmic noise and delightful devotion
Hide the non-linguistic urge to live!
Mother wants the blood of her child?
The blood frozen to be a devotional mark
On each and everyone's forehead.
The next to come is still chewing bread!
Blood trickles down from the world map
The whistling river is quivering red flood
Before the altar of Humanity!
Body overpowers the soul
Rituals overpower spiritual
Brutality overpowers humanity
Religion shatters realization!
The deadly sins are burning in the crematorium
We still nurture enemies in our inner emporium!

# The Second Coming

The earth becomes heavy with grief
'The center cannot hold' the warmth
Of coldness, of invisible war between
Head and heart, gentleman and gentle man,
Friend and fiend, look over and overlook!
Man lives in the chiaroscuro corner of life.
The Creator has turned out to be Destroyer
The Lamb of God won't act as a Protector
'The ceremony of innocence', a hyperreal cover

'The falcon cannot hear the falconer'!
The meditative Man of calmness dances fiercely
Plates get removed, the earth is quaking heavily

'A vast image out of Spiritus Mundi troubles my
sight'
The arrow of lust makes the meditative Man
open His sight!
The Second Coming! A new beginning!
The severe Heat is drowned in torrential raining.

# To Be or Not to Be

'To be or not to be, that is the question'
The 'undiscovered country' is beyond
apprehension!
The temple of the soul is crushed in inhuman
violation
That girl is quivering, sobbing in isolation!
The snake has left its skin to be His garland
The caterpillar becomes heavenly butterfly
The body becomes polluted, not the inner land
Leave the 'waste land' to fly high in the sky.
War goes on within without any invasion
Man has achieved everything, satisfaction?

# Innocence and Experience

Happy, the black boy could scarcely cry
'weep! weep! weep!'
Skin is besmeared with the chimney soot
The place of their sleep!
Going away from the desired destination
Happy is there losing his happiness
No Angel has come to sanctify his name
No God as Father to save his childhood.
You cannot match the rhythm of the poetry
Hyperreal comes in posing as reality!

The string of life has been broken
Experience proceeds to tame the innocent!
Happy, the black boy could scarcely cry
'weep! weep! weep!'
Tinsels here and there make the room dry
The right place to sweep!

# Heart-Mind Liaison

The heart is crossing gradually
The abyss, creation
Of the mind.
Painful panic
Pathetic path
Devouring like an inhuman.
I am a human
Hold tightly to the subtle thread
Of the heart
Stop suffering start struggling
The mind gets scared and

Flies away–
My vision is clear now.

# Solitude

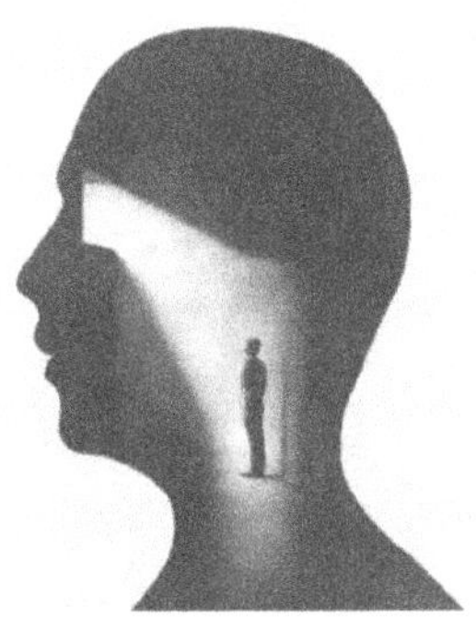

'Forlorn' rings a knell in the front door–
The hustle bustle is tenoring high
Like the smoke in a cigar
Twirling upwards
Only to meet death.
The 'self' suffers in isolation
It is necessary for realization
Still suffering —
We still have to grow.
The Banyan tree standing alone
Gripping and spreading its roots
The Eagle flying alone
Overcoming the thunder and storms
The sun shines after a bewailing moan
Everyone is fighting his battles alone.

Darkness is nothing but the absence of light
In the storm, 'the kite' takes a new flight
The curse of loneliness creates an inner feud
'Forlorn' rings a spell to know the 'self' in
solitude.

# The Veil

The fog veils the mountains and hills
The mist covers, uncanny prevails!
The costume is a veil to hide the body
The body is a veil to hide the skeleton
Gentility is a veil to hide the gentleman!
The intellect gets hijacked by the emotion
No key to lock the overflowing passion
War breaks out in outer and inner dimensions
The little atom has caused severe destruction!

Real is kept hidden under the labyrinthine veil of
hyperreal illusion
The busy human is too lazy to remove the veil to
attain enlightenment.

# The Screen

The child is staring at the screen
Digital rays are reflecting in his eyes
He is static, his fingers dynamic–
Sitting lazily scrolling the screen
The playful child is calm and cool
The child has lost its quality of playfulness!
Jack has become a dull boy
The new passion flows with digital toy
The afternoon ground is empty–
Greenery no more, an infertile heath!
The last ray is swallowed up in the clouds
Life begins, rotates, and ends on screens!
Darkness seeps into the diverted mind
'Brave new world' for the future mankind?
Can the children be the fathers of mankind?
The screen binds up, becomes a farsighted blind!

# The Pain of the Land

The designed development is kissing the sky
The 'bright star' in the smog heaves a sigh!
'The star to every wand'ring bark' lost its glitter
The tempest shatters the ship, sunk in dark
water!
The great sandwall is standing tall in the fertile
land

Postmodern builds up rapidly to be great and
grand!
The superman has lost his potential to be a
'Man'
Can 'Ong Sancti' restore the peace in wakeful
waste land?
The heat is increasing and the warmth
decreasing
In the fertile land, the weeds are still growing!

# Innocent Purity

Playing with the kids
Crescent smiling
Crippling minds heavy
With sudden grief
His father is dead!
Infant he is.
Night comes in morning
Sun hides in gloominess
One golden face among the swollens
Standstill in the yard
Innocent he is.
"Why father sleeping mumma

Tell him to bring apples for me"
Mother's heart breaks the silence of wife's–
Wise men are silent spectators
Child he is.
Bamboos are ready to carry
And fire to welcome
Water to reduce the pang
Air to balm!
Smile sprouts in toothless face
Kids come to play with–
Pure he is.

# The Truth

Truth is beauty and beauty truth
"Satyam Shivam Sundaram," the ultimate truth.
I don't have any desire to fit in the situation
Not wish even to walk in the crowd!
Don't listen to my 'self' for the sake of others
We've come alone, how can we die together?

Used again and again, never use my 'self'
Eyes are illusion! Heart keeps invaluable
wealth!
Never realized the importance of 'I'
The fertile land still remains dry!

Time flies away, pleasure is bed-ridden
Realize only the profit, ultimate loss is in
self-realization!

# Indoctrination

It's written on the wall – "Don't throw the plastic
cups here!"
The educated tea-lovers make garbage of
plastics there!
The conscious Wall appeals– "Don't pee here!"
The unconscious man reacts – "Right place
there!"
The educators celebrate Vivekananda's birthday!
Hue and cry speech, a far cry is a heyday!
They water the tree on a rainy day
The lonely tree suffers and dies on a sunny day!
The horse is running rapidly wearing blinkers
Rat race is on, cold war among educators!
Modern education is a reflection of hyperreal
simulation

Collective unconscious intensifies, products of
Indoctrination!

# The War

Third World War is approaching
Destruction is hovering around
Stuffy weather in the dark corner of the mind
Thunder, lightning, and bloodshed!
The enchanting melody of the flute gone by
The smiling flute player is holding the divine
discus
The field of Kurukshetra is ready for warfare
Satan's indomitable spirit vanishes in the air.
Kurukshetra war is going on continually within
Have you made Him the Charioteer to win?
The logical men can't hold the threads of
humanity
Torn into pieces, gentlemen would find peace in
divinity?
The world is suffering from viral fever
The viral postmodern warmonger – an achiever?

# Education

'Education is the manifestation of perfection
already in man'?
The educated gentleman becomes everything
except 'gentle man'!
Everyone is netted in the mechanical cobweb
The immortal bird is shivering in the golden
cage!
They discuss global warming in AC Rooms
Love is being sanctified in private rooms!
The glorious spirit has built the 'pandemonium'
The luciferous beauty confounded in satanic
delirium!

Harmony evaporates from the decorated
harmonium.
Only 'Brutus is an honorable man'!
Complexity is the outcome of modern education
The cultured society heaves a euphoric life of
ease
The potential mask-man is contracted with
contagious dis-ease!

# Camouflage

An elegant speech on 'smoking causes cancer'
Delivered by the eloquent minister,
Motivated clappings fill the air of the sanitorium
That satisfied soul smokes a ring in the
emporium!
A promise of livelihood before the election
Promises are made only to be broken!
Modern Karna donates before the cameraman
Scapegoats are made only to become
businessmen!
'Look like the innocent flower, but be the
serpent under it'

The galloping ambition reverses the personality–
split!
The disorder camouflages into the hyperreal
world
War breaks out, the glory of human potential?

# Home

Torrential rain with storm shatters the nest
The 'bird' gets terrified, seeks a shelter to rest.
The entrails cover up from head to toe
The fight is on to be born, wiping out the blow!
Fire is breaking out in the
Hearts of intense urge
The queen is in charge of the throne and

The women are toyed with only
To sing of the dreadful dirge!

The cold body is forlorn in the playground
And the peaceful pieces in the refrigerator
And the scratched one in the educated seminar
room!
Is there any house to be called a home?
The soul is departing from its worldly home
The Waste Bengal thinks only medieval
barbarism
Cheap ministers chiefly contribute renaissance
humanism!
Blood dripping out from the blue wheel
Of the Indian Flag–
It is found in a deserted 'Dustbin'!
'Use Me' is the call for homecoming?

# Let Her "Khadga" Decide Their Karma

That girl was raped and murdered.
The voice of truth was strangled
The potential vanished in the air
Lied the motionless on the floor
The temple of the soul blood-smeared
Education casts a naked glance!
She wanted to treat people's ailments
Ailments in the society she wasn't aware of
Worked very hard so that people live at ease

Unaware of the maskmen's potential disease!
Is there none to hold the divine discus for
protection?
Postmodern era only postulates hyperreal
simulation!
Candlelight can't be the method of protestation!
Only a midnight march is enough for
desecration?
Kali Maa should be invoked within to eradicate
stigma!
Laxmi has tolerated enough, let her 'khadga'
decide their 'karma'!

# The Aboriginal Woman

That toothless smile of that little girl
That zigzag dancing across the road
That braided hair with a red ribbon
That white dress and the green bag
That black face with the rays of the sun
Set in the west in the long run.
Ten thousand dreams were in her eyes
Trickled down as rains from the skies
The aboriginal girl would read and write?
The Black would make her future bright?
A roll of laughter mocked at the air
The born maid would glorify the chair?

Indomitable spirit survives and becomes radiant
The sun rises from the thatched roof to become
the Indian President.